Shadows of Gold is about the Eureka Stockade, an iconic event in Australia's history.

READ about how the discovery of gold in Victoria led to the seeds of rebellion…

DISCOVER how the gold rush resulted in a population explosion and was to become Australia's greatest decade in people building with diverse communities and religions, different races, and different ideologies…

LEARN about the arrival of the British in Victoria, its catastrophic impact on First Nations people and how this irrevocably changed the lives of First Nations people…

FIND OUT why the gold miners with the discovery of gold in Victoria were politically powerless and stung by daily oppression…

READ about how the stage was set for one of the most dramatic episodes of Australia's history and the events that led to the Battle of Eureka Stockade…

and much more…

Gold! Hidden Stories of Australia's Past, Book 2

Shadows of Gold

Eureka and the Birth of Australian Democracy

Marji Hill

Published by The Prison Tree Press 2022

Copyright © 2022 Marji Hill

Copyright © 2022 Artwork and paintings by Marji Hill

"Eureka Stockade" Oil painting by Marji Hill in Art Gallery of Ballarat collection

"The Southern Cross Flag" Oil painting by Marji Hill in Art Gallery of Ballarat collection

Paperback ISBN: 978-0-6454834-2-0
EBook ISBN: 978-0-6454834-3-7

Editor: Eddie Dowd

 A catalogue record for this work is available from the National Library of Australia

The Prison Tree Press
Suite 124, 1-10 Albert Avenue
Broadbeach, Queensland 4218

https://marjihill.com
https://www.fastselfpublishing.com

All rights reserved. No part of this book may be reproduced, stored in a retrieval system, or transmitted in any form or by any means, electronic, mechanical, photocopying, recording, scanning, or otherwise, without the prior written permission of the publisher.

Disclaimer

All the material contained in this book is provided for educational and informational purposes only. No responsibility can be taken for any results or outcomes resulting from the use of this material.

While every care has been taken to trace and acknowledge copyright the publishers tender their apologies for any accidental infringement where copyright has proved untraceable.

Every attempt has been made to provide information that is both accurate and effective, however, the author does not assume any responsibility for the accuracy or use/misuse of this information.

THE SERIES
Gold! Hidden Stories of Australia's Past

Book 1
Gates of Gold:
The Discovery of Gold, its Legacy and its Contribution to Australian Identity

Book 2
Shadows of Gold:
Eureka and the Birth of Australian Democracy

Book 3
Gold and the Chinese:
Racism, Riots and Protest on the Australian Goldfields

Book 4
Ghosts of Gold:
The Life and Times of Jupiter Mosman

Book 5
Blood Gold:
Native Police, Bushrangers & Lawlessness on the Australian Goldfields

DEDICATION

To the children
of Eureka

TABLE OF CONTENTS

Chapter 1 — A Defining Event   1
Chapter 2 — Trail Blazing   7
Chapter 3 — Discovery of Gold   29
Chapter 4 — The Seeds of Rebellion   43
Chapter 5 — Chain of events   53
Chapter 6 — The Battle   73

Sources   87
Questions for Further Consideration   89

About Marji Hill   91
More Books by Marji Hill   97

ACKNOWLEGEMENTS

In the spirit of reconciliation, I acknowledge the Traditional Custodians of Country throughout Australia and their connections to land, sea, and community. I pay my respect to elders, past, present, and emerging and extend my respect to all First Nation peoples today.

In the spirit of reconciliation, my mission is to increase understanding between the First Nations and other Australians and to provide people from all over the globe some basic understanding of Australia's first people, their history, and cultures.

In my life have been fortunate to have had several mentors. Alex Barlow, my late partner, would always say to me "If you manage your time well, you can achieve everything you want in life." That started my quest into the world of time management and learning how to maximise my productivity.

John Foley, barrister, helped me to expand my vision and has inspired me to make possible what seemed impossible. Sherien Foley has always been there to challenge and kickstart me and I remember her words when I hit rock bottom with my work many years ago and she said to me "There's only one way to go and that's up!"

This current series of books about gold grew out of a brainstorming session I had with my old friend, Gail Parr, while staying with her and her husband, George Sansbury at Maryborough in Queensland. We thrashed out the concept and from this grew these five books.

I would also like to acknowledge the late and great Jim Lynch who introduced me to the Charters Towers gold story many years ago and to his, son, Mark Lynch, Chairperson of the Citigold Corporation, who has always supported and encouraged my creativity in relation to the gold story both in books and in art.

And finally, thank you Eddie Dowd, my backstop and mentor, who has helped me get my books into their final form and ready for publication.

Marji Hill

"Australian democracy
was born at Eureka."

Dr H. V. Evatt

Chapter 1 — A Defining Event in Australian History

The battle of the Eureka Stockade was not only a defining event in Australian history, it was iconic - an episode the significance of which has been hotly debated.

Mark Twain described the Eureka Stockade as a revolution "small in size; but great politically; it was a strike for liberty, a struggle for principle, a stand against injustice and oppression... It is another instance of a victory won by a lost battle." [1]

The Late Hon. Susan Ryan (1942 - 2020) former Minister in the Hawke Government and Age Discrimination Commissioner within

---

[1] Ryan, Susan (2012) Human Rights Commission
https://humanrights.gov.au/about/news/speeches/activism-and-reform-eureka-and-human-rights

the Australian Human Rights Commission held the view that the Eureka Stockade was "not just a minor colonial stoush; it was a victory for peoples 'rights that attracted attention around the world at a time, the mid-19th century, when many of today's democracies were yet to fight for and win their freedoms."[2]

In December 1854 gold miners at Ballarat in Victoria initiated an armed uprising and battled to defend their rights against colonial government and authorities. Their underlying principles were equality, fair treatment by the government, and the right to take part in the government process.

The gold miners built the Stockade; they took up arms; and, under their beautiful blue flag, the Southern Cross, they fought for their rights under the leadership of Peter Lalor, an Irish immigrant.

---

[2] Twain, Mark (1897) *Following the Equator, Road to Ballarat, Chapter XXIV*, Classical Bookshelf, 1897. At http://www.classicbookshelf.com/library/mark_twain/following_the_equator/23/

The battle was short. It was bloody. The miners were outnumbered by the soldiers and they lost. It was a military disaster.

The miners might have lost the battle but they won the war against injustice.

Australia's great statesman and advocate for human rights, Dr H. V. Evatt[3] declared that: "Australian democracy was born at Eureka."

The Eureka Stockade became an Australian legend, and a controversial one at that. While the establishment has often tried to downplay its significance as a minor, short-lived event and a protest without consequence other leaders like Ben Chifley (1885 - 1951), Labor Prime Minister, said "it was the first real affirmation of our determination to be masters of our own political destiny." [4]

---

[3] Bolton. G. C. (1996) "Evatt, Herbert Vere (Bert) (1894-1965)", Australian Dictionary of Biography, National Centre of Biography, Australian National University. At http://adb.anu.edu.au/biography/evatt-herbert-vere-bert-10131

[4] Quoted in FitzSimons, Peter (2013) *Eureka the Unfinished Revolution*. William Heinemann. Ebook.

In the longer term all of the gold miner's demands were met. They got

- fairer licensing
- political representation
- the right to vote
- Peter Lalor was elected to the state parliament in Victoria.

From the immediate miner's perspective, the Battle of Eureka was unsuccessful. But their courage captured attention around the world and that of the government.

The Eureka Stockade laid the foundation for many aspects of the democratic system that Australia has today - freedom of speech, the right to vote, and political equality.

Eureka became an Australian legend. Leah Murray[5] says the battle symbolised "what the Australian people need in a legend: nationalism, democracy, and most importantly a 'fair go'." The fearlessness of the miners who fought against the odds was

---

[5] Murray, Leah (2013) The Eureka Stockade: Birthplace of Australian Democracy https://historychallenge.org.au/wp-content/uploads/2013/12/Leah-Murray-Eureka-Stockade.pdf

something that appealed to the Australian people.

Eureka Stockade

"The arrival of the British in Victoria
irrevocably changed the lives
of First Nations people. Then it was the
discovery of gold
that dictated the course of history"

Marji Hill

Chapter 2 — Trail Blazing into Victoria

Ballarat was the epicentre of Australia's gold rush. It was here in 1854 that the gold miners fought for their rights against colonial government oppression.

Wadawurrung

> The Wadawurrung people lived according to the law laid down in the Dreamtime by the great Ancestral Spirit, Karringalabil.
>
> Karringalabil turned himself into a man and created Wadawurrung Country. He created the "plants, animals, waterways, mountains, people and time. Once he did this, he turned himself into a wedge-tailed eagle we now call Bundjil. Bundjil's lore states that we must take care of this Country and respect it, in turn, Country will take care of people, providing food and shelter. "
>
> Traditional custodians Deanne Gilson and Tammy Gilson

Gold! Hidden Stories of Australia's Past

Book 2

Ballarat was built on the lands of the Wadawurrung people. Their lands extended over 10,000 square kilometres on the western side of Melbourne including Geelong and Ballarat.

By the time that gold was discovered the Wadawurrung people had already been devastated by the British takeover of their lands. This was exacerbated by the population explosion when thousands of people descended on Ballarat to mine for gold.

The Wadawurrung people came close to being exterminated by the time of the gold rush in 1851. Only a few Wadawurrung remained.

Traditional custodians Deanne Gilson and Tammy Gilson [6] describe how prior to British incursion into traditional lands the Wadawurrung lived according to the law laid down by the great Ancestral Spirit, Karringalabil.

---

[6] SBS "Lawless and Disorderly
https://www.sbs.com.au/gold/lawless-and-disorderly/

Karringalabil "turned himself into a man" and created Wadawurrung Country. He created the "plants, animals, waterways, mountains, people and time. Once he did this, he turned himself into a wedge-tailed eagle we now call Bundjil. Bundjil's lore states that we must take care of this Country and respect it, in turn Country will take care of people, providing food and shelter. "

Within the space of just seventy years around 90 per cent of Wadawurrung people were wiped out.

Wright[7] estimates that prior to 1788 there were up to 3240 members of the twenty-five Wadawurrung language groups. By 1861 only 255 First Nations people remained.

Before the discovery of gold

On 19 April 1770 Captain James Cook reached the east coast of Australia. His instructions were to take the eastern half of the continent for the British crown.

---

[7] Wright, Claire (2014) *The Forgotten Rebels of Eureka*. Melbourne, The Text Publishing.

At Possession Island, off Cape York Peninsula in North Queensland, Cook took possession of the whole of the eastern coast in the name of King George III. Cook declared that Australia was *terra nullius*.

This meant that Australia was a land without people and that it was unoccupied and unowned. Therefore, the belief of the time was that the British could justify claiming the continent of Australia as theirs.

Prior to 1770 before European discovery and occupation the land that is now known as Victoria was home to the First Nations. These people had inhabited the land for thousands of years.

The English navigators Bass and Flinders who were based at the new colony on Sydney Cove briefly explored the coast in the region of Port Phillip in 1797. At that same time, the Victorian coast was occasionally penetrated by the notorious sealers and whalers, escaped convicts, and sometimes shipwrecked innocents.

Early incursions into Victoria

In 1801, a British ship commanded by Lieutenant James Grant anchored for a few weeks in Western Port Bay. He established crops and a dwelling on Churchill Island.

Late in 1803 Colonel David Collins established a settlement at Port Phillip designed as a British base against possible French intrusion. This was just inside the heads at what is now Sorrento.

It was also a refuge from bad weather for sealers as well as a secondary settlement for the increasing number of convicts arriving in Sydney.

There were difficulties. Among other things there was a lack of fresh water and there was conflict with the local First Nation inhabitants.

In 1804 Collins departed and he sailed to the Derwent River in Van Diemen's Land.

Apart from occasional incursions, Victoria remained relatively free of British incursions for the next thirty years.

One of the convicts at Collins military settlement escaped. This was William Buckley. Buckley made his way by boat to the western side of the Bay where he settled with local First Nation people and lived with them for thirty years.

The first incursion by land occurred in 1824. This was at the time when Martial Law had been declared in Bathurst in New South Wales, during the height of the conflict between the Wiradjuri people and the British.

At this time British men rode their horses across the Murray River onto the traditional lands of Victoria.

The leaders of this party were the explorers W.H. Hovell and Hamilton Hume.

British occupation

The occupation of traditional First Nation lands started in earnest in the mid-1830s.

The forerunners were Edward Henry and Henry Camfield. These two free settlers arrived at Portland Bay with four convicts and some sheep in 1834.

In 1835 the Port Phillip settlement came into being with the arrival of two separate parties under John Batman and John Pascoe Fawkner. They heralded the British takeover of Victorian lands like a juggernaut.

More than 1,000 British settlers had reached the Port Phillip District within three years. Then by 1841, there were over 20,000 and by 1851, when the colony of Victoria was proclaimed, 77,000 people from Britain, Europe and Asia were occupying Victorian land.

In the short space of just fifteen years the resistance of Australia's first people had been completely broken and its population very much reduced.

John Batman's Treaty

On 29 May 1835, a grazier and businessman, John Batman and his party sailed from Launceston and entered Port Phillip.

Early that year Batman formed an association which consisted of fifteen members. The plan was to establish a colony of their own in the Port Phillip area and engage in stock breeding.

Batman sought out First Nation traditional owners of the land in the Port Phillip area.

He negotiated a treaty. The idea was to allow members of Batman's association to settle on their land by mutual agreement rather than conquest.

This famous treaty ceded to John Batman 100,000 acres (40,000 hectares) on the southern shore of Geelong harbour and by a second deed 500,000 acres (200,000 hectares) around the present city of Melbourne.

Batman returned to Van Dieman's Land and tried to have his treaty approved by his own colonial administration.

In the meantime, John Pascoe Fawkner, sent an expedition to Port Phillip. He settled on the banks of the River Yarra opposite the site Batman had selected for a village.

The party that Batman had left at Indented Head arrived at the Melbourne site to find the Fawkner party was already in place.

Both groups appealed to the Governor of New South Wales, Sir Richard Bourke.

Bourke declared that any treaty with the original Australians was illegal. When he realised that he had no hope of preventing European settlement in the area, Bourke decreed that the land would be sold by auction.

Batman was given a valuable land grant at Geelong and no more was heard of the proposed treaties between the settlers and the first people.

Sir Richard Bourke moved rapidly to protect the British Crown's title to the land by right of conquest.

The colonial government of New South Wales refused to recognise Batman's treaty as legitimate. It was the only attempt by any of the newcomers to engage First Nations people in a treaty or transaction rather than simply claiming land outright by conquest.

Initially, the occupation of Victoria came not from Sydney but from Van Dieman's Land (Tasmania). The Derwent River military post had become a penal settlement on a scale even larger than Sydney.

Van Dieman's Land also attracted wealthy settlers and by 1835 the demand for good grazing land had outstripped supply.

Land seekers quickly headed to the mainland to claim more grazing land.

Trail blazing south

In 1836 Major Thomas Mitchell who was the then Surveyor-General in New South Wales set out from Sydney to blaze the trail of British expansion further south.

The arrival of the British in Victoria irrevocably changed the lives of First Nations people.

On 24 May 1836 when Mitchell's party was on the northern bank of the Murray River it encountered a group of almost two hundred local First Nation inhabitants.

Mitchell[8] decided to attack. He ambushed the unsuspecting people. As they tried to escape the fire by swimming across the river they were shot in the water and those who reached the other side were also gunned down.

This was a massacre. Mitchell named this site Mount Dispersion and was rewarded with a knighthood and elevated to the lexicon of British heroes.

Mitchell crossed the Murray River into Victoria. He journeyed in a south western direction and discovered the rich, fertile plains of western Victoria.

The British Crown established its presence in Victoria. Governor Bourke appointed Captain William Lonsdale as Chief Agent of Government, Police Magistrate and Commandant for the Port Phillip Region.

A military post with soldiers and colonial police was set up on the Yarra in 1936. Bourke

---

[8] Grassby, Al & Hill, Marji (1988) *Six Australian Battlefields: the Black Resistance to Invasion and the White Struggle Against Colonial Oppression.* North Ryde, NSW, Angus & Robertson, p. 49

ordered a town to be laid out and named it Melbourne.

The arrival of pastoralists spelt gloom and doom for the Victorian traditional First Nations way of life. They put up a resistance and fought to defend their lands.

The seeds of war had been sown and it became clear that the British were taking over the lands in Victoria. Initially, the First Nations who fought in defence of their country greatly underestimated the power of European firearms.

Their experience was bloody when they realised that the musket was more powerful than any spear, boomerang, club or other weapon that they had ever devised.

The British pattern of invasion and destruction was set.

First Nations

Before the invasion by the British, the First Nations had defined territories and they knew the boundaries of their traditional lands. They knew its physical features, its geography, animals, birds, fish and plants.

They looked after their lands and ritually cared for their country with ceremony, songs, stories and art.

But with the taking over of traditional lands by the British for farming, precious traditional cultures were almost destroyed. First Nations people fought to defend their country from the north to the south and from the east to the west.

Not one colony in Australia was immune from the resistance wars.

The First Nations people of eastern Australia bore the full brunt of the British occupation of their lands and it was they who were the first to experience the dispossession of their culture.

What took place in eastern Australia was repeated throughout the continent in Victoria, Tasmania, South Australia, West Australia, the Northern Territory and Queensland. There was no discussion with the First

Nations, no treaty, and tragedy continued to unfold.

First Nations

Before the invasion by the British, the First Nations had defined territories and they knew the boundaries of their traditional lands. They knew its physical features, its geography, animals, birds, fish and plants.

They looked after their lands and ritually cared for their country with ceremony, songs, stories and art.

But with the taking over of traditional lands by the British for farming, precious traditional cultures were almost destroyed. First Nations people fought to defend their country from the north to the south and from the east to the west.

The area that now comprises the state of Victoria was the homeland to 38 First Nations people.

Those who lived close to waterways and the ocean had access to plentiful food resources. There was plenty of protein either from the land or the sea. There was a rich variety of vegetable foods.

The daily task of hunting and gathering food would only take a few hours of "labour" each day. So daily life for the First Nations people prior to 1788 could easily be described as affluent.

In Victoria at Lake Condah, the Gunditjimara people established an extensive farming system to trap eels. This farming method included smoking techniques to preserve the eels.

They established an eel industry and traded with others as far away as South Australia and New South Wales. In return for the eels, the Gunditjmara got quartz and flint to make stone knives and other stone implements.

It was easy for the Gunditjimara to obtain their regular food supply which included not only eel but possum and kangaroo.

The Gunditjimara lifestyle was sedentary.

They built stone villages with U-shaped or semi-circular houses that had low stone walls. A number of these dwellings have been found in south-western Victoria around Lake Condah and Condah Swamp.

They didn't have to lead a nomadic lifestyle moving from campsite to campsite because the area was rich in food resources. The waterways teamed with eels which were smoked on hearths made of basalt rocks.

This image contradicts the stereotype of traditional First Nation Australians as being the lean, hungry nomad constantly on the move in search of food and water.

The decentralised power structure of the Victorian First Nations was similar to that of the rest of the continent which left them open to invasion and occupation.

Killing fields

By 1861 Victoria had a population of over half a million Europeans and Asians.

The history of Victoria from the early 1830s to the time of the gold rushes in 1851 over a period of two decades can only be described as an era of killing.

As First Nations people retaliated against the British takeover of their lands they were systematically eliminated.

The First Nations had little chance against the superior weapons of the British.

Their experience fighting against European weaponry was bloody and they came to realise that the musket was more powerful than any spear, boomerang, or club.

The Koorie Heritage Trust Inc. documents on a map the locations where First Nations people in Victoria were massacred in those two decades from the 1830s to the 1850s [9].

---

[9] Culture Victoria "Massacre map"
https://cv.vic.gov.au/stories/aboriginal-culture/indigenous-stories-about-war-and-invasion/massacre-map/

In 1833-34 anywhere up to 200 deaths were reported in a massacre that happened at Portland. Known as the Convincing Ground Massacre, Gunditjmara people were massacred by British settler whalers.

Year after year massacre after massacre is documented as the British took over the lands of the Victorian First Nations people.

This frontier violence resulted in thousands of First Nations people dead.

One really shocking bloodbath was the Jack Smith massacre[10] at Warrigal Creek in 1843. Around 150 to 170 Brataualang people were killed over five days in retaliation for the killing of one single person — Ronald Macalister. He was the nephew of a local British squatter.

This was not a one off incident — this type of reprisal happened many times.

---

[10] Creative Spirits "Massacres: the frontier violence that's hard to accept"
https://www.creativespirits.info/aboriginalculture/history/massacres-the-frontier-violence-thats-hard-to-accept

Nathan Sentance [11], a Wiradjuri librarian and essayist, who examines Australian history refers to the work of Professor Lyndall Ryan who documented 270 frontier massacres over 140 years of Australian history which were systematic and organised attempts to eradicate First Nations people.

The brutality of the invasion and colonisation in Victoria, as occurred also in the rest of Australia, can only be described as near genocide.

Violent conflict on the Australian frontier started on this continent soon after the arrival of the First Fleet in 1788. From this time on, Australia experienced constant warfare on its frontier. This continued right up to the early 1900s with the last massacre of the first people being recorded in 1928.

In 1850 the British Parliament passed an Act for the setting up of the new colony of Victoria. In 1851 the colony of Victoria was

---

[11] Sentance, Nathan (2020) "Genocide in Australia" https://australian.museum/learn/first-nations/genocide-in-australia/

proclaimed with Charles Joseph La Trobe as its lieutenant governor.

It was the discovery of gold, however, that then dictated the course of history in Victoria.

First Nations people in Victoria were dispossessed in the name of the British Crown on the basis of *terra nullius*, meaning a continent a land without people.

The growth of the village on the Yarra was dramatic and the invasion of south-eastern Australia swift.

The Western District of Victoria had been penetrated and the traditional lands had been overrun by more than 300,000 sheep.

From this time on the Victorian countryside became full of people and their herds. A drought in the Monaro region of New South Wales after 1841 sent people and livestock flooding across the Murray River into northern Victoria.

This invasion of people was overwhelming. Thousands of people were pouring into Victoria.

They had no legal title to land at all under British law and of course none under the law of the First People.

"The rapid growth of the gold economy
had an irreversible effect
on both the landscape
and First Nations cultures."

Marji Hill

Chapter 3 – Discovery of Gold

People were flooding into Victoria but it was the discovery of gold that dictated the next phase of history in Victoria.

The separation of New South Wales from the Port Phillip District happened in 1850 with the colony of Victoria being proclaimed in 1851 with Charles La Trobe as its lieutenant governor.

The city of Melbourne came into being in 1847 followed by the incorporation of Geelong in 1849.

Gold

The first official discovery of payable gold in Victoria was in 1851 near Clunes. James Esmond in June of that year is credited with finding markable gold on Cresswick's Creek a tributary of the Loddon River.

There is some evidence that First Nations people and settlers had discovered gold prior to the find by James Esmond.

Because gold seekers were going north in droves to the newly discovered goldfields in New South Wales the government in Victoria offered an incentive to find gold in Victoria.

A reward of £200 was offered to anyone finding gold within 200 miles of Melbourne.

This triggered further discoveries at Ballarat, Castlemaine and Bendigo.

The historic gold rush at Ballarat occurred in August 1851. From this time to 1860 the Victorian goldfields which produced 25 million ounces of gold became the focus of attention in Australia.

Its discovery at Ballarat had sparked Victoria's famous gold rush and in its first year, an estimate of around 80,000 immigrants landed in Victoria. They came from different countries speaking many languages and practising many different religions.

Dreams of gold had for a long time dominated the Australian psyche. Gold fever had already gripped Sydney with the news of gold in California.

In January 1849 six ships crowded with people lured by gold sailed from Australia for San Francisco. By the end of that year many from Australia had joined the Californian gold rush.

The Australian gold rush that started in 1851 resulted in a population explosion and this era was to become Australia's greatest decade in people building.

Not only did gold seekers flock to the goldfields but along came administrators to run the new Victorian government.

Law and order

To maintain law and order on the goldfields La Trobe relied on his black mounted police force, which he sent to patrol the diggings and inspect the mining licences. The black police were known as "Joes" as their official police authorities were signed "Charles Joseph La Trobe".

Members of this Native Police Corps were the first police on the Ballarat goldfields. They arrived on the goldfields in 1851 under the command of Captain Dana.

They accompanied the officers on their rounds and effectively took action when needed to maintain law and order.

Early in 1849 prior to the official discovery of gold the Native Police Corps was dispatched to Daisy Hill. It had to guard a site where gold had been discovered on crown land.

One of the duties of the Native Police Corps was to escort the convoys of gold or prisoners from the goldfields back to Melbourne.

Not long after the discovery of gold at Ballarat, Gold Commissioner F. C. Doveton announced that the government was going to introduce a gold mining licence fee.

This unpopular decision inflamed the miners and was to lead to the rebellion known as the Eureka Stockade.

From this time on the Native Police Corps had a challenging time as they had to enforce this despised government decision.

This presence of a Native Police Corp angered the miners. They condemned it.

Already angered by the licence system, they were also upset by the high-handed and tyrannical tactics used by Dana and his police troopers. It got to the stage that Dana even had to call for reinforcements to help control the festering anger of the miners.

By May 1852, First Nations troopers started leaving the Corps and Dana was having trouble attracting new recruits.

Some of his black troopers returned to their families or went to work on pastoral properties. There were some who even went to the goldfields themselves to dig for gold.

The Native Police Corps was disbanded soon after Dana died on 24 November 1852.

Ballarat goldfields

In Wathawurrung country, the stage was set for one of the most iconic episodes in Australia's history.

Working the diggings was difficult[12]. Thousands of miners operated within a confined space.

The sides of the creek were congested with miners. They couldn't cross it without asking someone to make way.

Shafts up to forty-five metres deep had to be sunk and very often they filled with water that seeped through the porous soils. Pumps run by steam engines were used to keep them dry.

To operate mines like this, miners formed companies of ten to twenty, working in shifts to pump out the water. When the going was tough, companies often did not have even enough money to buy bread with their shafts only half finished.

Huge quantities of gold, including nuggets, were found in both deep and shallow

---

[12] Grassby, Al & Hill, Marji (1988) *Six Australian Battlefields: the Black Resistance to Invasion and the White Struggle Against Colonial Oppression.* North Ryde, NSW, Angus & Robertson, p. 209.

diggings. But there were many claims that did not produce any at all.

The claims were so small that violent arguments broke out over only a few centimetres of dirt.

A claim had to be worked for a minimum of a few hours every day and if not worked for twenty-four hours, it could be taken over by someone else. If a miner worked a sterile claim and then tried to switch to another, his neighbours could jump either his old one or the new one because he was not permitted to have two.

In the event of disputes, the Goldfields Commissioner was assisted by four assessors from among the miners who were supposed to adjudicate. Given the rivalry and tensions of the time most disputes were settled by the pick or the gun, or by the threat of them.

Multicultural melting pot

Educated and uneducated men and women from all over the world, be they artisans, priests, pastors, soldiers, convicts and even

First Nations people, were caught up in the prospecting golden frenzy.

Mining for gold offered people hope, the hope for a better life. The prospect of wealth and prosperity was the stimulus for families to leave their countries and embark on life-changing adventures on the goldfields.

The goldfields attracted people from all over the world and they came to live together in one giant multicultural melting pot. There was a mix of different ethnicities, different religions and different ideologies.

Many of the miners from Britain had been associated with the Chartist movement for political reform during the 1830s and 1840s. Then there were those who had been involved in the anti-authoritarian revolutions of Europe in 1848.

The majority of gold seekers came from England, Scotland, Wales and Ireland. There were the Cornish tin miners.

The multicultural melting pot included Chilean farmers and Africans; there were even soldiers from Mexico. Other countries were represented - Germany, the Netherlands, Denmark, France, Hungary, Poland, Italy, Canada and America. Some came from New Zealand and the Pacific. The largest non-European group were the Chinese.

The common denominator was gold. They all wanted gold.

Within months of the gold rush, Ballarat could boast a street of traders, stores, public houses, butchers, bakers, a chapel, and musicians. Tents were occupied by one or two miners or sometimes by whole families.

First Nations on the goldfields

The land on which the First Nations people lived and the country they looked after for thousands of years was now suddenly occupied by miners and their families.

Wathawurrung people were displaced and pushed from their country though some became active participants in the gold rush.

The traditional lifestyles of the Victorian First Nations people had been disrupted. Herds of cattle and sheep had adversely impacted the environment and now the miners rushing to the goldfields were scarring the landscape.

The rapid growth of the gold economy had an irreversible effect on both the landscape and First Nations culture.

Trees were cut down. Wood was being used for fires, to reinforce tunnels, and to build houses and shops. Waterways became polluted, the land was pitted with holes.

Fred Cahir in his book *Black Gold* [13] writes extensively about the role First Nations people had on the goldfields and their contribution to the new gold economy.

The Wathawurrung people in the Ballarat area in their effort to survive had to take on many roles undertaken by European settlers. These included mining, fossicking, and tracking.

---

[13] Cahir, Fred (2012) *Black Gold: Aboriginal People on the Goldfields of Victoria, 1850-1870*. Canberra, ANU E Press, p.1

> **First Nations people actively participated in gold mining displaying an entrepreneurial spirit and eagerness to participate in gold-mining and related activities.**

First Nations people actively participated in gold mining displaying an entrepreneurial spirit and eagerness to participate in gold mining and related activities.

They figured significantly in the golden era.

Some even looked after the children of the Eureka miners during the Eureka Stockade. Wathawurrung people it is believed took care of the Eureka rebels 'children at Black Hill in 1854[14].

---

[14] Cahir, Fred, ibid p.70

There are anecdotal accounts of First Nations people coming across gold nuggets even though there is no evidence that they attached any great economic or spiritual significance to the gold.

There are references to their being involved in gold mining. The goldfields had an attraction. Some First Nations individuals were motivated by factors such as new wealth, new sights, new sounds and new alliances.

Relationships were forged between many miners and First Nations people on the goldfields.

Their traditional knowledge, a knowledge well beyond the scope of most Europeans, was vital and greatly assisted the miners.

A notable skill of First Nations people was tracking. They could read the landscape, and interpret it. Their ability to act as guides in this so-called "new" country was indispensable.

First Nations people helped gold miners navigate their way in the country particularly if lost and they provided assistance to those who had run out of food or water.

Wathawurrung people helped miners cross waterways, helped them to prepare temporary shelters, and they acted as diplomats or interpreters.

"The miners were stung by daily oppression.
They realised
that they were politically powerless. They had
no vote
and no say at any level of government
yet they were subject to the tax."

Marji Hill

Chapter 4 – The Seeds of Rebellion

In August 1851 Lieutenant Governor La Trobe announced a monthly tax of thirty shillings. This tax was to be imposed on those working on the goldfields.

Goldfields Commissioner Doveton was despatched to Ballarat from Melbourne. He was accompanied by a contingent of troopers and armed police.

On 20 September he announced that fifteen shillings was immediately payable for what remained of the month. Then thirty shillings was to be paid on 1 October and monthly thereafter.

The reaction was swift.

Miners were struggling to find money to buy tools and supplies. Many could not pay the tax or else they found the fee a hardship. They believed that no licence tax would be payable until October.

The miners were outraged particularly given the tiny claims that they were allowed to work.

Protest

The miners held a protest meeting, shocked at the licence tax.

They were angry.

A delegation went to Doveton seeking a postponement of the tax until October. They also asked for a larger, allowable claim size [15].

Given the solidarity of the miners and their well-armed numbers, Doveton was persuaded to abandon the idea of collecting licence fees until October.

In December, La Trobe proclaimed that licence fees would be doubled to three pounds a month in the new year. This was to

---

[15] Grassby, Al & Hill, Marji (1988) *Six Australian Battlefields: the Black Resistance to Invasion and the White Struggle Against Colonial Oppression.* North Ryde, NSW, Angus & Robertson, p.214.

apply not just to those mining for gold but to anyone involved on the goldfields.

La Trobe came under attack from the press and was accused of appointing his minions to positions of power. The Goldfields Commissioner was accused of corruption.

There were protest meetings, attracting thousands of concerned people not only in Ballarat, Bendigo and Castlemaine but also in Melbourne. The Melbourne meeting resolved that the miners had a right to be consulted on the tax after all their numbers made up half the colony.

To ensure that miners paid the tax La Trobe ordered regular "digger hunts." These were sweeps by soldiers and the Native Police Corps to check licences. Many miners were driven off or arrested and sometimes even wounded as they resisted.

Spirit of rebellion

The spirit of rebellion quickened. In August 1853, around 3,000 miners grouped together in Ballarat to hear the report of a delegation

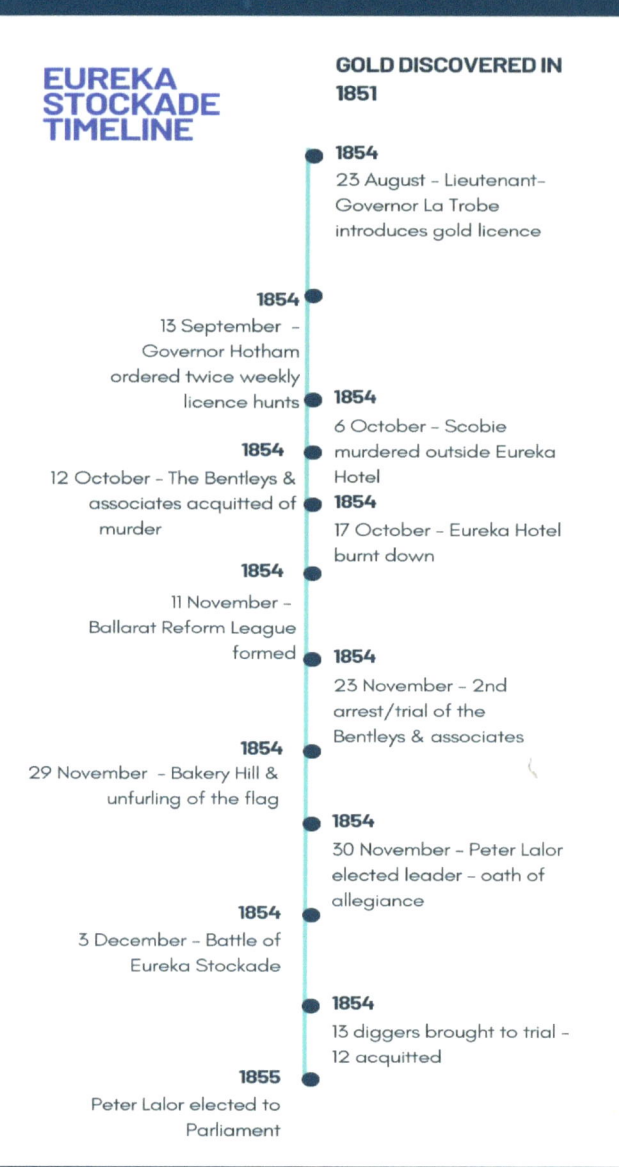

Gold! Hidden Stories of Australia's Past

Book 2

which had presented La Trobe with a petition protesting against his tax.

The protesters marched to the meeting in groups carrying their national flags.

La Trobe took fright at the extent of the opposition to taxation without representation. In November 1853 he proposed to the Legislative Council that the licence fee be abolished and that it be substituted by an export duty on gold.

The suggestion was flatly rejected by the council but the tax continued at a reduced rate of twenty shillings a month[16].

In June 1854 Sir Charles Hotham was appointed Lieutenant-Governor of Victoria before becoming Victoria's first governor.

At this time the colony was still in a ferment of hostility.

In August of that year, Hotham decided to visit Ballarat and show the flag. The miners were misled into thinking he was bringing

---

[16] Grassby, Al & Hill, Marji, *ibid* p.216.

them a change in policy. But they were to be disillusioned.

British soldier

Hotham failed to mention goldfields reform in his first speech to the Legislative Council. In addition, in an attempt to overcome a shortfall in colonial revenue, he ordered in September that monthly raids by the military and police to inspect licences be increased to twice a week.

Hotham was warned by Colonial Secretary Foster, Chief Commissioner Rede at Ballarat, Goldfields Chief Commissioner Wright and Chief Commissioner of Police MacMahon that confrontation was growing daily and becoming very bitter.

The colonial administration spent its time enforcing an unjust tax. At the same time needs such as roads, and crime prevention was ignored. Law and order were breaking down.

A man had been murdered and thrown down a mine shaft, a boy was left to drown in a creek, horses were stolen on a daily basis, and there were regularly nightly hold ups. Robberies and drunkenness was routine and there was mounting evidence of police corruption.

In addition to the breakdown of law and order there were challenges on the goldfields.

Surface and alluvial gold were exhausted. Miners had then to dig deep shafts and worked underground in appalling conditions.

They had to find the money to purchase special equipment and machinery and to tide them over the months when there were no returns at all.

Many were facing starvation and the digger hunts simply added to their misery.

There was the added insult that they were being taxed without representation or consultation and not even being accorded basic justice.

Melbourne had been in the grip of a financial crisis since 1853. Land owners and merchants who dominated the Legislative Council combined to avoid taxes and duties themselves and sought to shift the burden to the miners.

There was no doubt that the miners saw the British presence and administration as deliberately exploiting them [17].

---

[17] Grassby, Al & Hill, Marji, *ibid* p.218.

The miners were stung by daily oppression. They realised that they were politically powerless. They had no vote and no say at any level of government yet they were subject to the tax.

Again and again, at protest meetings, there was rage wherever the miners gathered. There was the catch cry "No taxation without representation".

The spirit of rebellion was abroad.

"The seeds of rebellion had been sown with the military raids, the government oppression,
the hounding of the diggers and the corruption,."

Marji Hill

Chapter 5 – Chain of events

On the night of 6 October 1854 a Scotsman, James Scobie, was murdered outside the Eureka Hotel. This started a chain of events that led to the Eureka Stockade.

Eureka Hotel murder

It was after midnight when Scobie wanted a drink at the bar of the hotel. He was told that the bar was closed but he demanded to be served. He was refused admittance.

Scobie protested and there was a violent altercation. Scobie was killed having been struck by a blow to his head from a shovel believed to have been wielded by the hotel owner, James Bentley.

Bentley, his wife Catherine and Thomas Farrell were arrested for the murder. They were found not guilty by police magistrate

John D'Ewes, a friend and business associate of Bentley.

This was seen by the diggers to be just another instance of government corruption.

This exoneration led to widespread protests. The mob was angry and the miners took matters into their own hands.

On 17 October 1854 several thousand diggers held a mass meeting to express their dissatisfaction. A committee was set up to seek the reopening of the legal proceedings against the Bentleys and to offer a reward for the identification and conviction of Scobie's murderer.

After the meeting, the mood turned ugly and a group of miners moved off to the Eureka Hotel. Passions ran high. In their fury Bentley's hotel was attacked, rocks were thrown, it was demolished and set alight.

The hotel was burnt down and the Bentleys and their associates only escaped with their lives with the help of the police.

Twenty-two year-old Catherine Bentley at the time was seven months pregnant. She was one of just over 5,000 women who resided at Ballarat.

Eureka Hotel is burnt down

On 19 October the Bentleys together with their associates, William Hance and John Farrell were arrested again and had to stand trial for Scobie's murder.

Hotham, the lieutenant governor, immediately despatched a few hundred police and soldiers from the 2nd Somersetshires, the 40th Regiment, to reinforce the military at Ballarat.

They were instructed to find the ringleaders who destroyed the Eureka Hotel. On 21 October Andrew McIntyre, Thomas Fletcher and Westerby were arrested and charged for leading the riot and burning down the Eureka Hotel.

On 1 November another mass meeting of diggers was held. The meeting received complaints about the corruption and about the torture by the police of a handicapped Armenian, Joannes Gregorius, who was a servant of Patrick Smyth the local Catholic priest.

The seeds of rebellion had been sown with the military raids, the government oppression, the hounding of the diggers and the corruption.

Ballarat Reform League

In late October 1854, the Ballarat Reform League began to take shape. This organisation rapidly became the driving force in the politicisation of the diggers and on 11 November it came into existence.

Its inauguration had bands playing and the various national flags from countries around the world were flown.

It condemned the regular violations of personal liberty and the law enforcement at Ballarat.

Thousands of diggers listened to the speeches which outlined the oppression, the atrocities and the corruption. The speakers called for political rights and reform. The Ballarat Times described the League as "the germ of Australian independence".

The Ballarat Reform League drew up a political manifesto[18] calling for the rights of the people and full Parliamentary representation. The meeting condemned government oppression and demanded the removal of the sergeant-major of the British regiment who they said had perjured himself to convict the three diggers of the Eureka Hotel riot.

---

[18] Grassby, Al & Hill, Marji (1988) *Six Australian Battlefields: the Black Resistance to Invasion and the White Struggle Against Colonial Oppression.* North Ryde, NSW, Angus & Robertson, p.225.

The manifesto drafted democratic principles, and wanted fair representation in parliament, manhood suffrage, removal of property qualifications for members of the Legislative Council, salaries for Members of Parliament and fixed parliamentary terms.

By 23 November 1854, the Bentley retrial had been concluded. Catherine Bentley was acquitted but Bentley and his associates were convicted of manslaughter.

On 25 November Andrew McIntyre, Thomas Fletcher and Westerby were convicted and sent to prison for their role in burning down the Eureka Hotel.

A delegation from the Ballarat Reform League met Hotham on 27 November demanding a pardon for the three diggers but this ended badly with Hotham being incensed and throwing the delegation out.

Seeds of rebellion everywhere

A detachment of troops from the 12th regiment arrived from Melbourne at the end of November 1854. When this news reached

Ballarat the first digger militia was quickly formed to intercept them.

The British troops, commanded by Captain H. C. Wise, brought cannon.

Diggers rushed the convoy overturning one wagon, capturing another and shooting several soldiers and an escort driver. The regimental drummer boy, John Egan, was wounded.

The British troops retreated to their military camp. Another detachment of troops was sent out to pursue the rebels.

When the troops attempted to enter the diggings, they were met by missiles and gunfire. The troopers drew their swords and cut their way back to the security of the camp in which they were rapidly becoming besieged.

That same evening a group of Reform League leaders met to discuss the new direction of the movement from the constitutional reform of the League to the proclamation of independence and the formation of a new directorate to carry forward the now inevitable armed struggle.

The meeting was presided over by a young Irishman named Peter Lalor (1827-1889).

Eureka flag

At this meeting, leaders agreed that there should be a flag, a symbol.

The design was suggested by Captain Charles Ross from Toronto in Canada and he was the first to die defending it.

While the council of war continued, three women, purportedly English, toiled through the night to produce a flag [19].

In another version of the events, again purportedly, one of the women was Irish, Anastasia Hayes, wife of Timothy Hayes. Another was Anne Duke, also Irish, while the third was Anastacia Withers, English.

---

[19] Wright, Claire (2014) *The Forgotten Rebels of Eureka*. Melbourne, The Text Publishing, p. 328.

The Southern Cross Flag

The silk flag with the blue ground had a large silver cross.

The next day there was a Monster Meeting on Bakery Hill to hear of the report of the delegation to Hotham. A stage and flagstaff were erected beneath which Captain Ross stood, sword in hand, surrounded by his rifle division.

At 11am on 29 November the Southern Cross flag was raised, still seen today as the symbol of Eureka, democracy and defiance.

It was 2pm when Timothy Hayes called on George Black to give his report. As he rose to speak he was greeted with cheers as one of the founders of the Reform League. It was the description of Hotham's rejection of the delegation that set a new dark mood.

Peter Lalor worked on a strategy the night before and he proposed that a new Central Committee be elected.

The digger militia had already been formed and it had seen action against the British troops the night before.

The Southern Cross, the flag of independence, had been unfurled. And now Lalor was proposing the establishment of a provisional government.

The next speaker was Raffaello Carboni who supported Lalor's call for a provisional government. He called on the diggers to salute the Southern Cross flag as the symbol of the oppressed.

Frederick Vern, from Germany, called for the abolition of all licences. The resolution was carried.

The decision was followed by volleys of rifle fire and pistol shots, fires were lit, and licences burned.

The challenge

Reaction from the government authorities was swift. Hotham issued orders to stand firm and reminded Commissioner Rede that he could call on the military, the police and the civil power.

The next morning on 30 November Rede ordered his forces onto the diggings to check for licences. As soon as the police reached the field and gave orders for the now non-existent licences to be produced, the digger militia came forward to resist.

Commissioner Rede read the riot act which gave the Crown the right to suspend any right of protest and order the dispersal of any assembly.

As he finished reading the signal was given for the troops to advance. Diggers retreated in all directions. Rede seized eight of them and charged them with not having licences.

The digger leadership acted quickly in the face of what amounted to a declaration of war.

It was led by the Reform League leaders: Peter Lalor, Raffaello Carboni, Frederick Vern and Captain Ross. A further general assembly on Bakery Hill was called at 3pm that same afternoon.

The Southern Cross flag was hoisted and once again Peter Lalor's voice boomed over the crowd as he called them to arms.

Holding a rifle with his left hand he mounted a stump and called on the diggers to fall into divisions behind their captains to prepare for war. His call was answered by a cry of unanimous acclamation and an army of 500 immediately formed up.

Kneeling down Lalor received the salute of the captains of each division and then, with his right hand pointing to the Southern Cross flying in all its glory in the afternoon breeze, proclaimed:

> "We swear by the
> Southern Cross to stand
> truly by each other and
> to fight to defend our
> rights and liberties" [20].

The diggers stretched out their hands to the flag and answered in unison "Amen".

---

[20] Grassby, Al & Hill, Marji (1988) *Six Australian Battlefields: the Black Resistance to Invasion and the White Struggle Against Colonial Oppression*. North Ryde, NSW, Angus & Robertson p.225.

We swear by the Southern Cross

Later that afternoon, Father Smyth came to propose a deputation to the military camp to demand the release of the eight diggers taken that morning and to demand that the troops take no further action in the area. Carboni was appointed to accompany them.

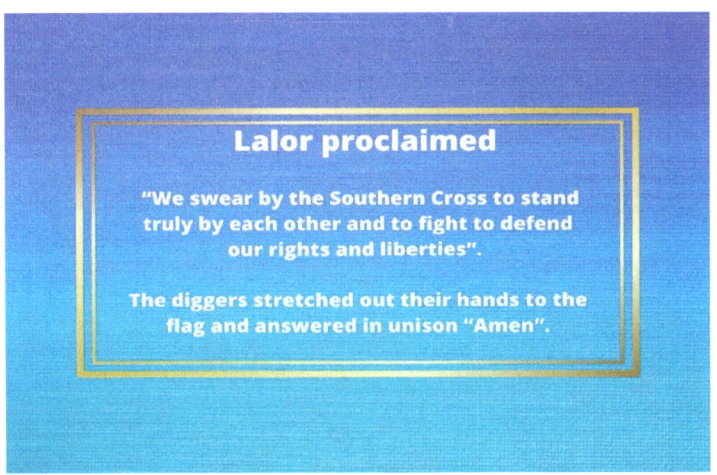

Commissioner Rede was challenged by the deputation. Incensed, he roared back at it declaring his authority and accusing them of strong democratic agitation by an armed mob.

Building the Stockade

Early on Friday, 1 December, the army of the Australian revolution began to assemble. The 500 or so men who had taken the pledge on Bakery Hill swelled to 800 and increased to 1,000 by the time they marched to Eureka.

Preparations were underway for the coming battle. Under the leadership of Frederick Vern, the rebel headquarters were established on approximately forty hectares of mining claims and miners' huts.

The Stockade was an area enclosed with mining slabs, logs, and other materials. The countryside was scoured for arms and ammunition. A blacksmith made pikes and barricades were built.

News of the planned rebellion spread rapidly and several hundred diggers arrived from Creswick.

The colony was aflame and all eyes were turned to the democratic capital of Ballarat.

Council for the Defence

Peter Lalor called a meeting of leaders. Twelve men made up the council of war. There was Peter Lalor, Raffaello Carboni, Frederick Vern, Edward Thonen, Timothy Hayes, Patrick Curtain, John Manning, Captain Ross, Captain Nealson, George Black and his brother Alfred, and Captain Nelson.

The meeting inaugurated the Council for the Defence and Lalor was elected provisional President.

Carboni, as Lalor's deputy, moved around the stockade spreading the word about Lalor. The authority of the president and the commander-in-chief and the revolutionary council was respected throughout Ballarat and news of its formation spread to neighbouring towns and settlements.

The government forces decided to set up a post on the Eureka field itself but Captain Ross and his men attacked driving the force back to their own camp and capturing arms and ammunition

News of the rebel's activities reached Hotham in Melbourne and a regiment was ordered to leave for Ballarat.

Activity at the stockade continued and the Council for the Defence was in almost constant session.

There were reports of reinforcement troops on their way from Melbourne. Captains Ross and Nealson rode out with their divisions to try to intercept and ambush them before they reached Ballarat but they were unsuccessful.

On Saturday 2 December, Father Smyth came to the stockade to address the diggers. He told them that the British strength in the military camp was 700 or 800 and that they were well armed and well equipped.

During the afternoon 200 men of the Independent Californian Rangers' Revolver Brigade swung into the stockade. Their arrival was a shot in the arm to the rebel force.

The Stockade was alive with rumours of a pending British attack. Security was tightened and the Council leaders instituted a password. This was "Vinegar Hill" which commemorated the Battle of Vinegar Hill which happened outside Sydney just fifty years before.

The rebel forces were potentially formidable and quite capable of challenging the British but their dispersal following the attempted ambush left inadequate numbers to defend the Stockade headquarters.

Hotham knew that if the battle against the rebels was lost in Ballarat, British power in Melbourne would be lost.

The British authorities made decisions that provoked rebellion. The repeated reports of opposition to the colonial rulers led them not only to anticipate a battle but to see it as inevitable and indeed a desirable way of suppressing dissent once and for all.

"Gold dust gave way to blood lust as the Eureka line became a killing field"

Claire Wright

Chapter 6 — The Battle

In 1854 on that fateful dawn of 3 December, Chief Commissioner Rede handed over the command of the colonial military force to Captain John Wesley Thomas, together with responsibility for the strategic battle plan.

Thomas had seen experience in India.

In the wee hours of Sunday morning, he assembled his forces for a surprise attack on the Stockade. He marshalled his 276 troopers consisting of mounted men and foot soldiers. They moved silently out of their camp.

By 4am just before dawn they had covered the 2.4 kilometres to the Stockade. Before this advance was discovered the regiment had taken up position close to the rebel camp.

Disaster was about to strike.

The digger forces had been reduced and weakened because their American detachment had been sent out to search for and intercept the troops that were coming in from Melbourne. Others had been dispersed to collect food and ammunition.

Of the 2,000 armed miners, only about 200 remained in the rebel Stockade that Saturday evening - the night before.

The Stockade

Captain Thomas was well aware that the rebel forces had been seriously depleted.

Lalor had not entertained the possibility that the colonial military would be bold enough to move out of its camp and head for the Stockade when it did.

He was focussed on a possible attack coming from the detachment on its way from Melbourne and this reinforcement was not due until Monday, 4 December.

When the diggers became aware of what was about to happen, Captain Thomas gave the order to advance but he instructed his men not to open fire until they heard the bugle. The British force moved forward to within metres of the rebels and very quickly the battle was on.

There were immediate casualties. An American commander from the rebel camp was wounded, and Captain Ross responsible for creating the concept of the Eureka flag was shot defending it.

Captain Wise of the colonial force was shot as he led his force over the stockade. The military bugle sounded the charge.

As soon as the diggers realised that an attack was about to happen Peter Lalor took charge and he rallied his forces at hand.

Seen silhouetted against the rising dawn, Lalor was shot. He fell to the ground his shoulder shattered.

Captain Ross was dead.

Thonen fought on until he was shot in the head.

Those diggers on the Stockade fortress stood their ground with their pikes against the military but they were cut down by sword and bayonet.

Thomas O'Neil, an Irish digger, badly wounded fought on to defend the flag, swinging his pike around his head until he was blown to bits with repeated gun fire.

Hafele, the German blacksmith who was responsible for making many of the pikes, kept fighting until he was felled.

Among those who fought to the last was the black American rebel, John Joseph. He had managed to survive as the British force charged through the Stockade bayoneting the wounded and venting spleen on the Southern Cross flag.

The Southern Cross flag was by now partly destroyed by bullets, stained with blood, torn down and desecrated.

Father Smyth moved into the stockade, ministering to the dying until he was dragged away by the troops intoxicated with their victory.

The Stockade was set alight.

The battle of Eureka was short in duration lasting only fifteen or twenty minutes. Reports of the number of diggers that died vary — anywhere between sixteen and sixty diggers were killed. Another dozen or so men and women were victims, many were wounded, and several would later die.

Others were gunned down by the troops and police. It was the bayonets that did the real damage.

There was mayhem and carnage. The British forces thrust their blades into the dead, the dying, and the wounded [21].

---

[21] Wright, Claire (2014) *The Forgotten Rebels of Eureka*. Melbourne, The Text Publishing, p. 375.

Women assisted the men and risked their lives to aid the wounded and the dying.

Lalor was badly wounded. One of his compatriots hid him until he was taken unconscious to the house of the Catholic priest, Father Smyth. The priest brought in some doctors who amputated his left arm.

Eventually, he was smuggled out of Ballarat and taken to the home of his fiancée in Geelong where he was operated on for another bullet wound to his side.

Four of the British force were killed and a dozen were wounded.

Wright says "Gold dust gave way to blood lust as the Eureka line became a killing field"[22].

Aftermath

On 6 December Governor Hotham declared martial law on the goldfields. This, however, was repealed several days later. Rewards

---

[22] Wright, *ibid*, p. 376.

were offered for the capture of the surviving rebel leaders.

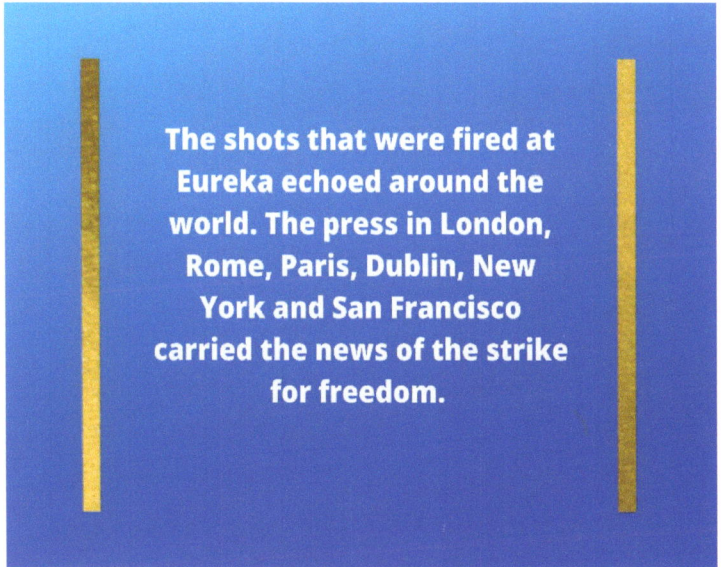

The shots that were fired at Eureka echoed around the world. The press in London, Rome, Paris, Dublin, New York and San Francisco carried the news of the strike for freedom.

The New York Times on 24 March 1855 was full of the "rebellion of the Southern Cross." The report ended with a stirring tribute to the diggers and the hoisting of the Southern Cross.

A report in Italy referred to the "Insurrection in Australia". The Italian press spread the news that the Australians who had hoisted the Southern Cross flag had been engaged in a bloody struggle against the British troops.

Despatches in Sri Lanka announced that the Australians had risen and declared their independence and that the British troops had put down the insurrection.

At the time Britain was engaged in the Crimean War but six of its morning newspapers gave coverage to the event that took place in Australia. They described the battle of Eureka, the proclamation of martial law, and reported that 10,000 citizens of Melbourne had assembled to review events.

Alarm bells rang loud and clear in London despite Hotham's report that the Battle of Eureka had been won, that Ballarat was no longer the democratic capital, that Lalor was wounded and in hiding with a price on his head and that 160 rebels were held prisoner.

Pressure from the United States, exerted through its consul general in Melbourne, made sure that not one American rebel was prosecuted. London, faced with unremitting hostility from the mass of people in the colony, abruptly dropped all charges.

Most rebels were released within a few days but several were held for months awaiting trial. Thirteen diggers were charged with high treason. Twelve were acquitted.

Within three years universal manhood suffrage was introduced and property qualifications for members of the Legislative Assembly were abolished.

Lalor emerged with one arm to contest the first election under the new law that gave diggers parliamentary representation. He was elected without opposition on 10 November 1855 to represent Ballarat in the Victorian Legislative Assembly.

The following year he was elected to the newly created Legislative Assembly for North Grenville and in 1859 he transferred to South Grant. In 1871 he was defeated but he regained his seat in 1875.

During nearly twenty-five years in parliament Lalor served as Postmaster General and Speaker of the Parliament.

The Battle of Eureka had been lost but many rights were won.

Those killed at Eureka did not die in vain. They laid the foundations of democracy in an independent Australia.

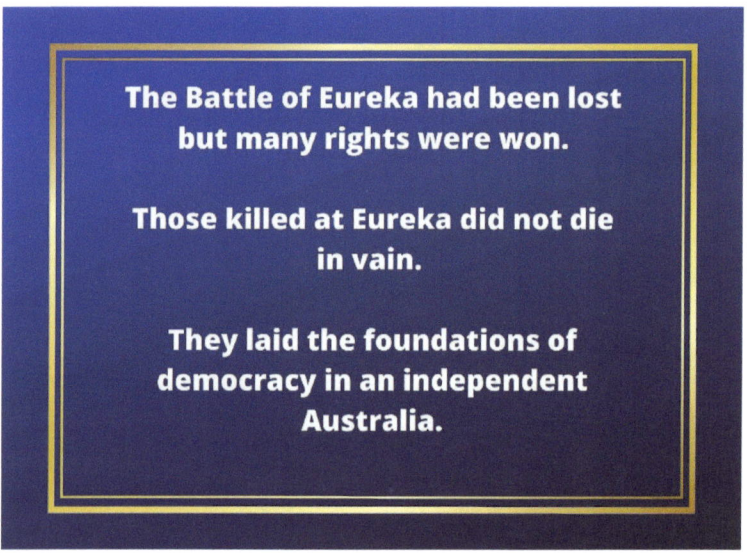

The Southern Cross was retrieved by an English trooper, John King. It was kept by the King family until it was obtained by the Ballarat Fine Art Gallery in 1895.

The flag was restored and in 1973 it was unveiled by the then Prime Minister, Gough Whitlam, who saluted the men of Eureka with the words:

> "The Eureka Stockade became an Australian legend.
>
> The events of 3 December 1854 remain in the memory and consciousness of Australians"

Dr H. V. Evatt, the great statesman and perceptive historian, went so far as to declare that: "Australian democracy was born at Eureka" [23].

---

[23] Grassby, Al & Hill, Marji (1988) *Six Australian Battlefields: the Black Resistance to Invasion and the White Struggle Against Colonial Oppression.* North Ryde, NSW, Angus & Robertson, p.238.

Gold! Hidden Stories of Australia's Past

Book 2

And now...

In the next book in this series, *Gold and the Chinese: Racism, Riots and Protest on the Australian Goldfields,* we will uncover the reality about Australia's relationship with the Chinese, how they migrated to the goldfields like thousands of others from all parts of the world and got caught up in the golden frenzy of prospecting for gold.

Sources

The author acknowledges the following sources of information:

Bolton. G. C. (1996) "Evatt, Herbert Vere (Bert) (1894-1965)", Australian Dictionary of Biography, National Centre of Biography, Australian National University. At http://adb.anu.edu.au/biography/evatt-herbert-vere-bert-10131

Cahir, Fred (2012) *Black Gold: Aboriginal People on the Goldfields of Victoria, 1850-1870.* Canberra, ANU E Press

Creative Spirits "Massacres: the frontier violence that's hard to accept" https://www.creativespirits.info/aboriginalculture/history/massacres-the-frontier-violence-thats-hard-to-accept

Culture Victoria "Massacre map" https://cv.vic.gov.au/stories/aboriginal-culture/indigenous-stories-about-war-and-invasion/massacre-map/

FitzSimons, Peter (2013) *Eureka the Unfinished Revolution.* William Heinemann. eBook.

Grassby, Al & Hill, Marji (1988) *Six Australian Battlefields: the Black Resistance to Invasion and the White Struggle Against Colonial Oppression.* North Ryde, NSW, Angus & Robertson.

Murray, Leah (2013) "The Eureka Stockade: Birthplace of Australian Democracy" https://historychallenge.org.au/wp-content/uploads/2013/12/Leah-Murray-Eureka-Stockade.pdf

Ryan, Susan (2012) Human Rights Commission https://humanrights.gov.au/about/news/speeches/activism-and-reform-eureka-and-human-rights

SBS "Lawless and Disorderly" https://www.sbs.com.au/gold/lawless-and-disorderly/

Sentance, Nathan (2020) "Genocide in Australia" https://australian.museum/learn/first-nations/genocide-in-australia/

Twain, Mark (1897) *Following the Equator, Road to Ballarat, Chapter XXIV*, Classical Bookshelf, 1897. At http://www.classicbookshelf.com/library/mark_twain/following_the_equator/23/

Wright, Claire (2014) *The Forgotten Rebels of Eureka.* Melbourne, The Text Publishing.

Questions for Further Consideration

How did the Eureka Stockade influence today's Australia?

What were some of the anti-authoritarian revolutions that spread across Europe prior to the discovery of gold in Australia in 1851?

What does it mean to fly the Eureka flag today?

About Marji Hill

Artist & Author

Marji Hill, artist and painter since childhood, runs her art career alongside her career as an author.

Marji is a highly respected international author as well as a seasoned business executive, researcher, and coach.

She is passionate about promoting understanding between Australia's first people and other Australians.

Marji has fostered the spirit of reconciliation in all her writings since she was Research Fellow in Education at the Australian Institute of Aboriginal and Torres Strait Islander Studies (AIATSIS) in Canberra.

From 2008 to 2011, Marji was Deputy Chairperson of the Mosman Branch of Reconciliation Australia in Sydney.

Following her Education Research Fellowship at AIATSIS in 1976 Marji, together with her late partner, Alex Barlow, produced more than seventy (70) books on all aspects of the First Nations people including the critical, annotated bibliography *Black Australia*.

In 1989 Marji was the Project Coordinator and one of the researchers and writers of *Australian Aboriginal Culture* the official Australian Government publication on First Nations people.

In 1988 her work of non-fiction *Six Australian Battlefields,* which she co-authored with Al

Grassby, was published by Angus and Robertson. A decade later it was re-published by Allen & Unwin as a paperback edition.

Her nine-volume encyclopaedia, *Macmillan Encyclopaedia of Australia's Aboriginal Peoples* was published in 2000 and in 2009 she published *The Apology: Saying Sorry To The Stolen Generations.*

Marji's more recent publications extend to self-improvement and self-help with books like *Staying Young Growing Old* and *Inspired by Country* a self-help book about painting with gouache.

Marji's artworks range from very large oil paintings on canvas (her largest being 213 x 167cm) to very small works on paper - gouache being a favourite medium.

Black/white relations, reconciliation, Eureka, and the discovery of gold are common themes not only in her writings but also in her art.

Her small paintings are simple responses to land and sea environments.

Painting has been a lifetime passion for Marji. She remembers as a child winning first prize for a painting she exhibited at the Southport agricultural show. Then in her teens for two years in a row she won the Sunday Mail Child Art Competition in Queensland with her winning paintings getting full coverage in colour in the newspaper.

Marji's formal art training took place in the 1980s at the Canberra School of Art which in 1992 became ANU School of Art & Design.

As soon as she completed her Master of Arts Degree in Anthropology at the Australian National University (ANU), Marji went on to get a Post Graduate Diploma in Painting. She has held eight solo exhibitions in Canberra, Melbourne and Sydney and she has participated in various group shows.

One of her large paintings was included in the 2004-2005 Ballarat Fine Art Gallery's Traveling Exhibition *Eureka Revisited: the Contest of Memories*. This exhibition travelled to Melbourne, Canberra and Ballarat — part of the 150-year celebration of the Eureka Stockade.

Two of her large paintings were commissioned by the Citigold Corporation. One did hang for many years in the foyer of Jupiters Casino in Townsville until the casino was sold, becoming The Ville Resort-Casino.

Jupiter's Lucky Strike celebrates the discovery of gold by First Nations boy, Jupiter Mosman in 1871 at Charters Towers in North Queensland. This painting today hangs in the offices of the Citigold Corporation in Charters Towers.

The other, a portrait of Jupiter Mosman resides in the World Centre in Charters Towers.

Marji's paintings are in many private collections both in Australia and overseas and she is represented in the Ballarat Fine Art Gallery and the Ballarat and Sydney campuses of the Australian Catholic University.

For many years Marji travelled extensively both within Australia and internationally, working as a consultant, doing speaking engagements, motivating people and developing her art career.

Marji has returned to her birthplace and now resides in Surfers Paradise, Australia. She pursues her interests in writing, painting, mentoring, publishing, and internet marketing.

More Books by Marji Hill

Self-improvement/Self-Help

Hill, Marji (2014) *Staying Young Growing Old.* Broadbeach, Qld, The Prison Tree Press.

Hill, Marji (2020) *How Big Is Your Why? An Author's Guide to Time Management and Productivity to Achieve Transformational Results.* Broadbeach, Qld, The Prison Tree Press.

Hill, Marji (2020) *A Create and Publish Toolbox: 101 Prompts In A Guided Journal To Help You Write, Self-publish, And Market Your Book On Amazon.* Broadbeach, Qld, The Prison Tree Press.

Hill, Marji (2021) *Inspired by Country: an Artist's Journey Back to Nature, Landscape Painting with Gouache.* Broadbeach, Qld, The Prison Tree Press.

First Nations

Hill, Marji (2021) *First People Then And Now: Introducing Indigenous Australians.* 2nd ed. Broadbeach, Qld, The Prison Tree Press.

Hill, Marji (2021) *Australian Aboriginal History: 5 Stories of Indigenous Heroes.* Broadbeach, Qld, The Prison Tree Press.

Gold

Hill, Marji (2022) *Gates of Gold: The Discovery of Gold, Its Legacy and Its Contribution to Australian Identity.* Broadbeach, Qld, The Prison Tree Press. (Gold! Hidden Stories of Australia's Past, Book 1)

Hill, Marji (2022) *Shadows of Gold: Eureka and the Birth of Australian Democracy.* (Gold! Hidden Stories of Australia's Past, Book 2)

Hill, Marji (2022) *Gold and the Chinese: Racism, Riots and Protest on the Australian Goldfields.* (Gold! Hidden Stories of Australia's Past, Book 3)

Hill, Marji (2022) *Ghosts of Gold: The Life and Times of Jupiter Mosman.* (Gold! Hidden Stories of Australia's Past, Book 4)

Hill, Marji (2022) *Blood Gold: Native Police, Bushrangers & Lawlessness on the Australian Goldfields.* (Gold! Hidden Stories of Australia's Past, Book 5)

Gold! Hidden Stories of Australia's Past

Book 2